31
Keys TO A New Beginning

BY MIKE MURDOCK

Wisdom is the principal thing; therefore get wisdom: and with all thy getting get understanding.

Proverbs 4:7

Wisdom International
P.O. Box 747
Dallas, Texas 75221

Unless otherwise indicated, all Scripture quotations are taken from the *King James Version* of the Bible.

31 Keys To A New Beginning
ISBN 1-56394-016-7
Copyright © 1994 by Mike Murdock
P.O. Box 99
Dallas, Texas 75221

Published By
Wisdom International
P.O. Box 747
Dallas, Texas 75221

WHY I WROTE THIS BOOK

Everything has to have a beginning . . . except the Beginning. God is the MASTER of New Beginnings.

He Loves beginnings.
He is is the Alpha and the Omega.
He is the Beginning and the End.

> He began life.
> He began earth.
> He began animals.
> He began people.
> He began events.
> He began the Universe.
> He began YOU.

Sometimes we make unfortunate mistakes.
Sometimes we make unwise decisions.
Sometimes we take devastating wrong turns in life.

We become damaged. Severely damaged. Suicidal thoughts dance across the stage of our mind, mocking sneering and defying us. Self-destruction seems a magnetic, compelling and even desirable option to our present mess we have created.

We need a New Beginning. A Second Chance.

That's why I've stayed in love with Jesus. He gives you a second chance.

That's why I wrote this book for You.

KEY 1

LISTEN TO PAIN.

Pain is discomfort created by disorder. It is not really an enemy. It is a signal, a memo, a messenger telling you an enemy exists.

- ❑ When you were a child, you may have touched a hot iron. It hurt! Pain made you jerk your hand away . . . make changes . . . to protect yourself from injury.

- ❑ If things are going wrong in your life, take it seriously. Pain talks. Initiate any change that may be necessary.

- ❑ You have already been in your past. It did not satisfy you, or you would have stayed there.

- ❑ It is time for changes. Big changes.

- ❑ Get back up. Don't stay down. It is time for a New Beginning.

————WISDOM WORDS————

"...Weeping may endure for a night, but joy cometh in the morning."   Psalm 30:5b

"Come now, and let us reason . . ."   Isaiah 1:18

KEY 2

DESPISE YOUR PRESENT CHAINS.

You are a child of the Most High God. Captivity is unnatural for you. Learn to hate the chains of any habit that enslaves you.

- ❑ While drug addicts and alcoholics may want the taste of sin, they certainly do not want the torment. But they will never be free until they learn to despise those chains.

- ❑ Habit is Hell's greatest weapon in destroying your life. Let God break your chains.

- ❑ What you can tolerate, you will not be able to change.

- ❑ So don't complain about the things you are permitting to go on in your life.

——— WISDOM WORDS ———

"The Spirit of the Lord God is upon me; because the Lord hath anointed me to preach good tidings unto the meek; he hath sent me to bind up the brokenhearted, to proclaim liberty to the captives, and the opening of the prison to them that are bound."   Isaiah 61:1

"If the Son therefore shall make you free, ye shall be free indeed."   John 8:36

KEY 3

KNOW YOUR OPPONENT.

Satan is your real adversary. He is a fallen angel, dispelled from heaven by a righteous God.

❑ His methods are predictable. He incites the violent nature of men against you. He inflames the normal passions of man into perversion. He introduces thoughts that could ultimately destroy you.

❑ He reacts to the spoken Word of God. He is easily demoralized with the Weapon of Praise. He flees when you resist him.

——————WISDOM WORDS——————

"Who shall separate us from the love of Christ? shall tribulation, or distress, or persecution, or famine, or nakedness, or peril, or sword? Nay, in all these things we are more than conquerors through him that loved us." Romans 8:35,37

"For we wrestle not against flesh and blood, but against principalities, against powers, against the rulers of the darkness of this world, against spiritual wickedness in high places." Ephesians 6:12

KEY 4

CONSIDER THE CONSEQUENCES OF REBELLION TO THE WILL OF GOD.

Rebellion is punished. Always. It may not happen today, but it is inevitable. Each seed of disobedience is like a magnet attracting tragedies into your life.

❏ God will never advance you beyond your last act of disobedience. Joshua learned this at the Battles of Ai, when Achan attempted a cover-up of his sin. The Israelites lost the battle.

❏ God is not stupid. He is not blind. He sees everything. Sooner or later . . . He reacts to it. You cannot afford the losses your rebellion will create.

❏ When you see an alcoholic or drug addict, you see someone who has lost the most precious things in life — his health, loving relationships, and self-confidence.

❏ God promises gain to the obedient. He guarantees loss to the disobedient.

❏ Every loser can be a lesson to us. LEARN.

————WISDOM WORDS————

*"Then shall they call on me, but I will not answer; they shall seek me early, but they shall not find me: For that they hated knowledge, and did not choose the fear of the Lord.
Therefore shall they eat of the fruit of their own way, and be filled with their own devices." Proverbs 1:28, 29, 31*

KEY 5

DO NOT ATTEMPT TO COVER UP YOUR MISTAKES.

E veryone has sinned against God. Publicly or privately.

- ❑ You are instructed in the Word to confess that sin and turn away from it. Do it now. Obey Him.

- ❑ Only a fool would attempt to deceive God. Your confession will unlock His mercy.

- ❑ Your weaknesses do not worry Him. He is not confused and bewildered about your deliverance.

- ❑ He is waiting for you.

- ❑ He knows the futility of sin. He is well acquainted with the empty promises of satan.

——WISDOM WORDS——

"For all have sinned, and come short of the glory of God;"
Romans 3:23

"For the wages of sin is death; but the gift of God is eternal life through Jesus Christ our Lord."   *Romans 6:23*

"He that covereth his sins shall not prosper: but whoso confesseth and forsaketh them shall have mercy."
Proverbs 28:13

KEY 6

RECOGNIZE YOUR DELIVERERS.

God assigns Deliverers. Moses was assigned to lead the Israelites out of Egypt. Elijah was sent to the widow of Zarephath to help her use her faith for provision.

❑ If you are sick, look for the man of God who believes in healing. If you are having financial problems, look for the man of God who believes in prosperity.

❑ No one fails alone. If you fail, it will be because you chose to ignore those God assigned to help you.

❑ Recognize messengers from God.

❑ When Satan wants to destroy you, he sends a person. When God wants to bless you, He sends a person.

❑ Recognize them. Whether they are packaged like a John the Baptist in a loincloth of camel's hair, or the silk robes of King Solomon.

❑ Your reaction to a man or woman of God is carefully documented by God. When God talks to you, it is often through the spiritual leaders in your life. Don't ignore them.

———— WISDOM WORDS ————

"He that receiveth a prophet in the name of a prophet shall receive a prophet's reward: and he that receiveth a righteous man in the name of a righteous man shall receive a righteous man's reward."   *Matthew 10:41*

KEY 7

CONFESS AND FORSAKE ANY KNOWN SIN.

G uilt is the Thief of Faith.

❑ When you permit sin in your life, you become uncomfortable in the presence of God.

❑ It is difficult to expect a miracle from a God you resent. Confess your failure. He forgives.

❑ Your mistakes and sins have not shocked God. He anticipated your need for mercy.

❑ The Master Key to Recovery is Repentance.

❑ Don't justify yourself. Quit blaming others for the decisions you have made. Repent. Immediately.

───── WISDOM WORDS ─────

"If I regard iniquity in my heart, the Lord will not hear me."
Psalms 66:18

KEY 8

NOW CELEBRATE YOUR NAME IN THE BOOK OF LIFE.

God keeps a daily journal. He records the names and victories of every one of His children.

❑ Overcomers will never be blotted out of His Book. The name of every overcomer will echo through the Chambers of Heaven. Angels will hear it.

❑ Get excited today about overcoming. You are stepping into the Arena of Champions. Your name is becoming familiar in Heaven these days.

―――――WISDOM WORDS―――――

"He that overcometh, the same shall be clothed in white raiment; and I will not blot out his name out of the book of life, but I will confess his name before my Father, and before his angels."   *Revelations 3:5*

KEY 9

EXPECT A TURN-AROUND AS A REWARD TO YOUR OBEDIENCE.

Today is not permanent. Your worst circumstances today are subject to change.

❏ God is stepping into the Arena of your life. He is turning the tide in your favor.

❏ You are never as far from a miracle as it first appears.

❏ Examine the rewards of obedience to God.

❏ Obedience is doing whatever God instructs you to do.

❏ Each instruction is linked to a miracle in your future.

❏ Each act of obedience shortens the distance to any miracle you are pursuing.

❏ Remember God only feels obligated to the obedient. The obedient always receive answers to their prayers.

───────WISDOM WORDS───────

"Every valley shall be exalted, and every mountain and hill shall be made low: and the crooked shall be made straight, and the rough places plain: And the glory of the Lord shall be revealed, and all flesh shall see it together: for the mouth of the Lord hath spoken it." Isaiah 40:4, 5

KEY 10

MAKE TODAY THE GREATEST EVENT OF YOUR WHOLE LIFETIME

Do not be passive today. You are ALIVE! Act like it!! Talk like it!! Celebrate yourself!!

- ❑ Speak a little louder today. Speak a little faster.

- ❑ Smile bigger . . . laugh aloud . . . and exude the joy of Jesus as you spread it generously over every single hour today.

- ❑ You have accepted Christ as your personal Saviour. *"The Word is nigh thee, even in thy mouth, and in thy heart: that is, the word of faith, which we preach; That if thou shalt confess with thy mouth the Lord Jesus, and shalt believe in thine heart that God hath raised him from the dead, thou shalt be saved."*

Romans 10:8-10

WISDOM WORDS

"This is the day which the Lord hath made; we will rejoice and be glad in it."   *Psalms 118:24*

KEY 11

GET MOVING TOWARD GOD AND HIS ASSIGNMENT FOR YOUR LIFE.

Y ou will never possess what you are unwilling to pursue.

☐ Race horses never win races while they are in stalls.

☐ God rewards reachers.

☐ Your enthusiasm will attract the right people in your life.

─────WISDOM WORDS─────

"The steps of a good man are ordered by the Lord: and he delighteth in his way."　　　*Psalms 37:23*

FIND THE PROBLEM GOD CREATED YOU TO SOLVE.

E verything God has made is a solution to a problem.

☐ Your worth and significance are determined by the kinds of problems you are solving for someone. If you want to earn $100.00 an hour, you must find a $100.00 an hour problem to solve.

☐ Your significance is not in your similarity to others. It is in your difference. Find your point of difference . . . and solve a problem with it. Prosperity is inevitable.

☐ One of the Master Keys to personal miracles is to get involved with the needs of others. Find your assignment.

☐ Joseph used his gift of interpreting dreams to calm a tormented Pharaoh. He was promoted from the prison to the palace. Job prayed for his friends during the worst crisis of his life. It released God to reverse the curse.

——WISDOM WORDS——

"Withhold not good from them to whom it is due, when it is in the power of thine hand to do it."   *Proverbs 3:27*

KEY 13

TELL SOMEONE WHAT JESUS HAS DONE FOR YOU.

The first two letters of the word "gospel" spell . . ."GO."

❑ Christianity is a network of activity. Promote Jesus today. He is the Starting Point of every miracle. Be the bridge that connects Him to somebody in trouble today.

❑ Be bold. One miracle is worth a thousand sermons.

❑ You are the creation. He is your Creator. You cannot out-think the One who made you.

❑ He has delighted in performing the Impossible. He has turned your sickness into health . . . poverty into prosperity . . . tears into laughter.

❑ He is the Master of the Turn-around.

❑ Jesus has made the difference in your life. Tell someone about it today.

———WISDOM WORDS———

"Go ye into all the world, and preach the gospel to every creature. And these signs shall follow them that believe; In my name shall they cast out devils; they shall speak with new tongues; They shall take up serpents; and if they drink any deadly thing, it shall not hurt them; they shall lay hands on the sick, and they shall recover." Mark 16:15, 17, 18

KEY 14

START PURSUING THE WISDOM OF GOD.

Wisdom is simply doing what God would do in a given situation.

❑ Wisdom is the Master Key to financial prosperity.

❑ Jesus is made unto us the Wisdom of God. Whatever you face today, just do what you know Jesus would do.

❑ Jesus said you have received two gifts from God: (1) Your mouth and (2) His wisdom.

❑ Unexpected things may happen today. Don't worry. The Holy Spirit within you will rise to the occasion and speak through you.

❑ Relax. Someone greater than you is within you. Depend on Him.

——WISDOM WORDS——

"Get wisdom, get understanding: forget it not; neither decline from the words of my mouth." Proverbs 4:5

"Length of days is in her right hand; and in her left hand riches and honour." Proverbs 3:16

KEY 15

FACE ANY PROBLEM HONESTLY.

Don't blame others for what you have chosen to do. Don't blame others for the consequences of your choices. Remember . . . never complain about what you permit.

- ❑ Your life is the result of your choices.
- ❑ Name your weaknesses. Nobody else can do it. Nobody else will do it. Nobody else should have to do it. Your honesty will determine your victories.
- ❑ Run toward the mountain you want to see moved, just as David ran toward Goliath when he cut his head off.
- ❑ Your open reach for God sets your new beginning in motion . . . TODAY.
- ❑ Life is a collection of battles. Subsequently, it is also a collection of victories.
- ❑ Reach down deep inside yourself today and call forth your greatest strength.
- ❑ Today is not a day for weakness. It is time to be tough.
- ❑ Be tough.

————WISDOM WORDS————

"If thou faint in the day of adversity, thy strength is small."
Proverbs 24:10

"A wise man is strong; yea, a man of knowledge increaseth strength."
Proverbs 24:5

KEY 16

WITHDRAW FROM CONTENTIOUS PEOPLE AND ABANDON ABUSIVE FRIENDSHIPS.

There are four kinds of people in your life: those who add, subtract, divide, and multiply.

❏ Those who do not increase you, inevitably will decrease you.

❏ It is the responsibility of others to discern your worth.

❏ A contentious person is a trouble-maker. He spreads discontent, frustration, and distrust.

❏ He gossips. He slanders. He promotes strife.

❏ Do not feed a relationship with such a person.

————WISDOM WORDS————

"Make no friendship with an angry man; and with a furious man thou shalt not go: Lest thou learn his ways, and get a snare to thy soul." Proverbs 22:24, 25

"As coals are to burning coals, and wood to fire: so is a contentious man to kindle strifes." Proverbs 26:21

17

KEY 17

CREATE A MIRACLE CLIMATE.

A tmosphere matters. An atmosphere of praise and worship can unlock your faith for miracles.

❑ When David played his harp for Saul, evil spirits departed from the palace. Anointed music is one of the master keys in creating a miracle-climate.

❑ Keep a cassette player handy. Use it to make a conscious effort today to keep godly music playing all day long.

❑ Listen to anointed music.

❑ Godly music drives evil spirits away.

❑ When depression enters, and the battle rages . . . turn on a music cassette that ushers in the Presence of God. Satan reacts to it. He fears it.

———WISDOM WORDS———

"But now bring me a minstrel. And it came to pass, when the minstrel played, that the hand of the Lord came upon him."
II Kings 3:15

"And it came to pass, when the evil spirit from God was upon Saul, that David took a harp, and played with his hand: so Saul was refreshed, and was well, and the evil spirit departed from him." *I Samuel 16:23*

KEY 18

ALLOW YOURSELF TIME TO CHANGE.

Don't be too hard on yourself. Little-by-little and day-by-day, you will start tasting the rewards of change.

☐ Look at the patience of God with Israel. He "knew they were but flesh." He took many years to even train their leader, Moses. You are not an exception.

☐ Every man fails. Champions simply get back up . . . and begin again.

☐ Give God time to work.

☐ Sometimes those things you desire the most may take longer to achieve. It takes longer to make a Rolls Royce automobile than a bicycle.

☐ Millions of Miracles have been dashed on the Rocks of Impatience. Give God time.

☐ Something good is happening that you do not see. Wait joyfully with great expectations.

————WISDOM WORDS————

"The Lord upholdeth all that fall, and raiseth up all those that be bowed down."   Psalm 145:14

"And let us not be weary in well doing: for in due season we shall reap, if we faint not."   Galatians 6:9

KEY 19

FEED YOUR FAITH DAILY.

Faith is your confidence in God. Sometimes it is weak or may even seem nonexistent. At other times, it may be powerful and incredibly strong. It depends on the food you feed it.

☐ Faith is a Tool . . . a Key . . . a Weapon. A tool to create a future; a Key to unlock God's Storehouse of Blessing; and the Weapon that defeats satan.

☐ Faith comes when you hear God talk. Listen today to His Spirit, His Servants, His Scriptures.

☐ Absorb the promises of God.

☐ Study the Covenant God established with those who walk in obedience to Him.

☐ You can only operate in faith according to your knowledge of His will or desire for your life. For example, if you do not know that God has already provided for your healing, how can you believe Him for a miracle in your health?

☐ You must have a clear photograph of the will of God so your faith can implement it.

————WISDOM WORDS————

"So then faith cometh by hearing, and hearing by the word of God."   *Romans 10:17*

". . . He that cometh to God must believe that He is, and that He is a rewarder of them that diligently seek Him."

Hebrews 11:6

KEY 20

BEGIN THE BIBLE HABIT.

Pick a time . . . preferably, the morning. Call it your "Wisdom-Hour." Read the Bible aloud.

❑ Don't get bogged down in theology, or the Greek and Hebrew translations. Just meditate on His Word.

❑ His Word is life. His Word creates faith. His Word will change the course of your life.

❑ Pour the Word over your mind daily.

❑ Your mind gathers the dirt, grime and dust of human opinion every day.

❑ Renew your mind to the TRUTH—God's Word. Schedule an appointment with the Bible daily. The renewing of your mind is the key to changes within you.

❑ The Words of God are like waterfalls . . . washing and purifying your mind.

——————WISDOM WORDS——————

"Study to shew thyself approved unto God, a workman that needeth not to be ashamed, rightly dividing the word of truth. But shun profane and vain babblings: for they will increase unto more ungodliness."

II Timothy 2:15, 16

21

KEY 21

MAKE PRAYER TIME AN APPOINTMENT.

Two unforgettable disciples, Peter and John, kept their prayer appointment with God.

❏ Daniel prayed three times daily. The psalmist prayed seven times daily. Great men simply have great habits.

❏ You make appointments with lawyers, doctors and friends. Start making appointments with God.

❏ Enjoy His presence.

❏ When you get into the presence of God, something happens that does not happen anywhere else.

❏ Bring to Him your fears, worries, doubts and tears. You greatly matter to Him today.

❏ So, enjoy Him. He certainly enjoys you.

─────WISDOM WORDS─────

"If ye abide in me, and my words abide in you, ye shall ask what ye will, and it shall be done unto you." John 15:7

"Thou wilt shew me the path of life: in thy presence is fullness of joy; at thy right hand there are pleasures for evermore."   Psalm 16:11

KEY 22

DISCERN GOD'S
DAILY AGENDA.

Your agenda (schedule for today) should be decided in the presence of God. Your daily agenda will create miracles or tragedies depending on whether or not you are led by the Spirit of God. HOURLY.

- ☐ Obedience is an hourly event.

- ☐ Your inner peace is a signal. Don't make a phone call, an appointment or a decision unless you are at peace in your heart about it.

- ☐ Remember . . . success is a daily event.

- ☐ Success is a daily event . . . called joy. It happens hourly when you do the Will of God.

- ☐ Habit is also a daily thing. Nothing will ever dominate your life unless it happens daily.

- ☐ Focus on today's priorities. A priority is anything God has commanded you to do today.

————WISDOM WORDS————

"For as many as are led by the Spirit of God, they are the Sons of God."   *Romans 8:14*

"It is the Lord's mercies that we are not consumed, because his compassions fail not. They are new every morning: great is thy faithfulness."   *Lamentations 3:22, 23*

KEY 23

ATTEND CHURCH FAITHFULLY.

G et into the Presence of God. Regularly. Your best will come out of you in His presence.

❑ Sit under the teaching of a man of God you respect. Put your time, influence and finances there, faithfully.

❑ Even Jesus attended church regularly. There is no substitute for the Golden Link of godly relationships.

❑ Network with others.

❑ Remember, one cannot multiply.

❑ Develop people skills. Listen, learn and absorb from others. Ask questions and document answers.

❑ Success is a collection of relationships. Whatever you are willing to settle for, determines the quality of your future.

————WISDOM WORDS————

"Not forsaking the assembling of ourselves together, as the manner of some is; but exhorting one another: and so much the more, as ye see the day approaching."
Hebrews 10:25

"As His custom was, he went into the synagogue on the sabbath day." *Luke 4:16*

"Two are better than one: because they have a good reward for their labor. For if they fall, the one will lift up his fellow: but woe to him that is alone when he falleth; for he hath not another to help him up." *Ecclesiastes 4:9, 10*

KEY 24

TITHE WITH AN EXPECTATION OF A 100-FOLD RETURN.

Tithe means "tenth." Abraham brought ten percent of his income back to God in thanksgiving for the blessing of God.

☐ This tithe is "Holy Seed."

☐ As you bring your tithe to God this week, wrap your faith and expectation around it and look for the promised harvest.

☐ Tithing is the Biblical practice of returning ten percent of your income back to God after you have earned it.

☐ In the Old Testament, Abraham tithed. In the New Testament, even the Pharisees' tithing was noted by Jesus.

☐ Make God your financial partner. Make every payday a Seed-Sowing Day. Results are guaranteed.

─────── WISDOM WORDS ───────

"Bring ye all the tithe into the storehouse, that there may be meat in mine house, and prove me now herewith, saith the Lord of hosts, if I will not open you the windows of heaven, and pour you out a blessing, that there shall not be room enough to receive it. And I will rebuke the devourer for your sakes, and he shall not destroy the fruits of your ground . . ."
Malachi 3:10, 11

25

KEY 25

LISTEN TO MENTORS OF FAITH.

Joshua learned under Moses. Timothy learned under Paul. Elisha learned under Elijah.

- ❏ Observe successful lives carefully. Secrets will surface. Reasons for their success will emerge.
- ❏ Read biographies of extraordinary people who tapped into the Fountain of Faith. Their lives will excite you to new heights of faith.
- ❏ Treasure your mentors.
- ❏ Your mentor is anyone who consistently teaches you what you want to know.
- ❏ Mentorship is accepting perfect knowledge from an imperfect man.
- ❏ Pursue and extract the knowledge of the mentors that God has made available to your life.
- ❏ You will never travel beyond your wisdom.

———— WISDOM WORDS ————

"Wherefore seeing we also are compassed about with so great a cloud of witnesses, let us lay aside every weight, and the sin which doth so easily beset us, and let us run with patience the race that is set before us." Hebrews 12:1

"A wise man will hear, and will increase learning; and a man of understanding shall attain unto wise counsels:"
Proverbs 1:5

KEY 26

ENDURE CORRECTION.

Wisdom begins with correction. Errors must be exposed. Mistakes must be admitted.

- ❏ Think back over your life. Think of the person who taught you the most. He was probably the one who corrected you the most.

- ❏ Hell is full of people who rejected correction. Heaven is full of people who accepted it.

- ❏ Learn to listen.

- ❏ Somebody knows something you do not know. That information may be invaluable. You have to listen to receive it.

- ❏ Something inside you may want to scream out for attention. You have a longing to be heard. Restrain yourself. Learn to listen.

- ❏ Remember, God talks. How often? As often as you need help.

————— WISDOM WORDS —————

"A wise man will hear, and will increase learning; and a man of understanding shall attain unto wise counsels."
                                        Proverbs 1:5

"For whom the Lord loveth He chasteneth, and scourgeth every son whom He receiveth. Now no chastening for the present seemeth to be joyous, but grievous: Nevertheless afterward it yieldeth the peaceable fruit of righteousness unto them which are exercised thereby." Hebrews 12:6, 11

27

RISK EVERYTHING TO BE AN OVERCOMER.

O vercomers are the Rewarded. In fact, they are the only ones who are rewarded through eternity.

❑ Even the Apostle Paul counted everything as loss except his position with Christ. Each victory authorizes God to promote you.

❑ In the World System, birth may decide rank. In the Kingdom System, battle decides rank. Every satanic attack upon you is simply another opportunity for promotion.

❑ Refuse to quit.

❑ The Secret of Champions is their refusal to quit trying.

❑ Futility is merely a feeling. Conquer it and keep heading toward your goals.

❑ Create small successes when the large ones seem impossible.

❑ Even skyscrapers are built a brick at a time.

—————WISDOM WORDS—————

"I have fought a good fight, I have finished my course, I have kept the faith: Henceforth there is laid up for me a crown of righteousness, which the Lord, the righteous judge, shall give me at that day: and not to me only, but unto all them also that love his appearing."   II Timothy 4:7, 8

KEY 28

WHEN YOU FEEL TROUBLED, REACH FOR HELP.

R eaching out for help is not a sign of weakness. So, do it.
Only a fool ignores a life jacket when he is drowning.

❑ Overcomers don't do it alone. They conquer their pride.
   They reject the trap of isolation. They reach. They
   know the inevitable reward of reaching.

❑ Turn to God. Honor those who are qualified to help
   you. Your future depends on it.

❑ Run to the refuge.

❑ Cities of refuge existed in Old Testament times. If a
   man was accused of a crime, he could run into a city of
   refuge and was guaranteed protection by law.

❑ You, too, have a Place of Refuge. When satan the
   accuser, brings accusations against your life, run
   to God.

❑ God responds to reachers. Stop looking at where you
   have been, and start looking at where you can be. Run to
   the Refuge. Do it today.

—————WISDOM WORDS—————

*"When thou art in tribulation, and all these things are come
upon thee, even in the latter days, if thou turn to the Lord
thy God, and shalt be obedient unto His voice; (For the Lord
thy God is a merciful God;) he will not forsake thee, neither
destroy thee, nor forget the covenant of thy fathers which he
sware unto them."* Deuteronomy 4:30, 31

KEY 29

DON'T PANIC WHEN TROUBLE STRIKES.

Something may happen today that shocks you. Don't worry about it. God anticipated it.

- ❑ Remember, satan is merely an ex-employee of Heaven. God knows him quite well. He fired him.
- ❑ Get alone today in the presence of God. Fear will die and courage will flourish.
- ❑ Analyze adversity.
- ❑ There are four ways to respond to a crisis: Maximize it. Minimize it. Advertise it. Analyze it.
- ❑ Maximizing . . . is to exaggerate the crisis.
  Minimizing . . . is to understate the crisis.
  Advertising . . . is to tell the whole world about it.
  Analyzing . . . is extracting useful information from it.
- ❑ Crisis is merely concentrated information. Adversity is simply your enemies' reaction to your progress. Taking the time to analyze it will benefit you.

───── WISDOM WORDS ─────

"Be still, and know that I am God . . ." Psalm 46:10

"In the days of prosperity be joyful, but in the day of adversity consider . . ." Ecclesiastes 7:14

KEY 30

KEEP WALKING.

Picture this. You are in your car. You are driving in a heavy hailstorm. You don't stop . . . but keep driving knowing you will move out of the storms range.

- ❑ Remember Joseph. Remember David. Every day of adversity was simply a stepping stone toward the throne.
- ❑ Keep walking.
- ❑ Remember, seasons change.
- ❑ Attacks don't last forever.
- ❑ People change. Weather changes. Circumstances change. So don't be discouraged today. Expect supernatural and dramatic changes.
- ❑ Tomorrow is coming. Your future is unlike any yesterday you have ever known.
- ❑ Jesus invested His first 30 years in preparation for His ministry. Moses spent 80 years becoming a great leader.
- ❑ Time is your friend. Don't hurry.
- ❑ Remember, Patience is the weapon that forces deception to reveal itself.

———— WISDOM WORDS ————

"Weeping may endure for a night, but joy cometh in the morning."   *Psalm 30:5*

"When thou passeth through the waters, I will be with thee; and through the rivers, they shall not overflow thee: when thou walkest through the fire, thou shalt not be burned; neither shall the flame kindle upon thee, for I am the Lord thy God. . ."   *Isaiah 43:2, 3*

31

KEY 31

KEEP THE SPIRIT OF A FINISHER.

Anyone can begin a marathon. Champions finish them.

- ❑ Everyone experiences adversity. It is those who stay strong to the finish who are rewarded.

- ❑ Pace yourself. Determine to "go the distance." Keep aflame the Spirit of a Finisher.

- ❑ Never, never, never give up.

- ❑ Your dreams and goals are worth any fight, any waiting, any price. Don't give up.

- ❑ Your perseverance demoralizes your enemy. Don't give up.

- ❑ Patience is a weapon. Don't give up.

——————WISDOM WORDS——————

"And Jesus said unto him, No man, having put his hand to the plow, and looking back, is fit for the kingdom of God."
Luke 9:62

". . .But he that endureth to the end shall be saved."
Matthew 10:22

Has embraced his assignment to pursue... possess... and publish the Wisdom of God to heal the broken in his generation.

Began full-time evangelism at the age of 19, which has continued for 30 years.

Has traveled and spoken to more than 12,000 audiences in 36 countries, including East Africa, the Orient, and Europe.

Noted author of 72 books, including best sellers, *Wisdom for Winning, Dream Seeds,* and *The Double Diamond Principle.*

■ Created the popular *"Wisdom Topical Bible"* series for Businessmen, Mothers, Fathers, Teenagers, and the *One Minute Pocket Bible.*

Has composed more than 5,400 songs such as *I Am Blessed, You Can Make It, Holy Spirit This Is your House, and Jesus Just The Mention Of Your Name,* recorded by many artists.

Is the Founder of the Wisdom Training Center, for the training of those entering the ministry.

Has a weekly television program called *"Wisdom Keys With Mike Murdock"* and daily radio *broadcast "The Secret Place.*

He has appeared often on TBN, CBN, and other television network programs.

Is a Founding Trustee on the Board of Charismatic Bible Ministries.

Has had more than 3,400 accept the call into full-time ministry under his ministry.

May I Invite You To Make Jesus Christ The Lord Of Your Life?

The Bible says, 'That if thou shalt confess with thy mouth the Lord Jesus, and shall believe in thine heart that God hath raised Him from the dead. thou shalt be saved. For with the heart man believeth unto righteousness; and with the mouth confession is made unto salvation." (Rom. 10:9-10)

To receive Jesus Christ as Lord and Savior of your life, please pray this prayer from your heart today!

"Dear Jesus, I believe that You died for me and rose again on the third day. I confess to You that I am a sinner. I need Your love and forgiveness. Come into my life, forgive my sins, and give me eternal life. I confess You now as my Lord. Thank You for my salvation! I walk in Your peace and joy from this day forward. Amen."

Signed _____

Date _____

Return this today!

☐ Yes, Mike! I made a decision to accept Christ as my personal Savior today. Please send me my free gift of your book *31 Keys to a New Beginning* to help me with my new life in Christ.

Name _____

Address _____

City _____ State _____ Zip _____

Phone(____) _____

Mail To:
Dr. Mike Murdock
P.O. Box 99 - Dallas, Texas 75221

Clip & Mail

Your Letter Is Very Important To Me

Y ou are a special person to me, and I believe that you are special to God. I want to help you in every way that I can. Let me hear from you when you are facing spiritual needs or experiencing a conflict in your life, or if you just want to know that someone really cares. Write me. I will pray for your needs. And I will write you back something that I know will help you receive the miracle you need.

Mike, please enter into the prayer of agreement with me for the following needs:

(Please Print)

_____

_____

_____

_____

_____

_____

_____

_____

_____

_____

_____

_____

_____

Mail To:
Dr. Mike Murdock
P.O. Box 99 - Dallas, Texas 75221

Will You Become A Wisdom Key Partner?

What Is This Ministry Involved In?

1. Television & Radio - "Wisdom Keys With Mike Murdock," a nationally-syndicated weekly television program features Mike Murdock's teaching and music. The daily radio broadcast, "The Secret Place", is reaching thousands.

2. WTC - The Wisdom Training Center where Dr. Murdock trains those preparing for full-time ministry in a special Training Program.

3. Missions - Dr. Murdock's overseas outreaches to 36 countries have included crusades to East Africa, Brazil and Poland.

4. Music - Millions of people have been blessed by the anointed songwriting and singing talents of Mike Murdock, who has recorded over 20 highly-acclaimed albums.

5. Literature - Best-selling books, teaching tapes and magazines proclaim the Wisdom of God.

6. Crusades - Multitudes are ministered to in crusades and seminars throughout America as Mike Murdock declares life-giving principles from God's Word.

7. Schools of Wisdom - Each year Mike Murdock hosts Schools of Wisdom for those who want personalized and advanced training for achieving their dreams and goals.

8. Schools of the Holy Spirit - Mike Murdock hosts Schools of the Holy Spirit to encourage, illuminate and mentor believers to the person, and companionship of the Holy Spirit.

I want to personally invite you to be a part of this ministry!

WISDOM KEY PARTNERSHIP PLAN

 Dear Partner,
God has brought us together! I love representing you as I spread His Wisdom in the world. Will you become my Faith-Partner? Your Seed is powerful. When you sow, three benefits are guaranteed: **Protection** (Mal. 3:10-11), **Favor** (Luke 6:38), **Financial Prosperity** (Deut. 8:18). Please note the four levels as a monthly Wisdom Key Faith Partner. Complete the response sheet and rush it to me immediately. Then focus your expectations for the 100-fold return! (Mark 10:30)

Your Faith Partner,
Mike Murdock

Yes, Mike, I want be a Wisdom Key Partner with you. Please rush The Wisdom Key Partnership Pak to me today!

❏ **Foundation Partner...** Yes, Mike, I want to be a Wisdom Key Foundation Partner. Enclosed is my first monthly Seed-Faith Promise of $15, as God makes possible.

❏ **Seed-a-Day...** Yes, Mike, I want to be a Wisdom Key Partner as a Seed-a-Day member. Enclosed is my first monthly Seed-Faith Promise of $30, as God makes possible.

❏ **Covenant of Blessing...** Yes, Mike, I want to be a Wisdom Key Partner as a Covenant of Blessing member. Enclosed is my first Seed-Faith Promise of $58, as God makes possible.

❏ **The Seventy...** Yes, Mike, I want to be a Wisdom Key Partner as a member of The Seventy. Enclosed is my first monthly Seed-Faith Promise of $100, as God makes possible.

Total Enclosed $ _____ #DC10

Name _____

Address _____

City _____ State _____ Zip _____

Phone _____ Birthday _____

37

Wisdom Key Partnership Pak

When you become a Wisdom Key Monthly Faith Partner, you will receive our Partnership Pak which includes:

1. Special Music Cassette
2. 101 Wisdom Keys Book
3. Partnership Coupon Book

Clip & Mail

Yes, Mike! I Want To Be Your Partner!

❑ Enclosed is my best Seed-Faith Gift of $_____

❑ I want to be a Wisdom Key Partner! Enclosed is my first Seed-Faith Gift of $_____for the first month.

❑ Please rush my special Partnership Pak. (#PP02)

Name _____

Address _____

City _____State _____Zip _____

Phone _____

Mail To:
Dr. Mike Murdock
P.O. Box 99 - Dallas, Texas 75221

Powerful Wisdom Books From Dr. Mike Murdock!

You can increase your Wisdom Library by purchasing any one of these great titles by God's voice of Wisdom, Mike Murdock. Scriptural, practical, readable. These books are life-changing!

 **The Covenant Of 58 Blessings**
Dr. Murdock shares the phenomenon of the 58 Blessings, his experiences, testimonials, and the words of God Himself concerning the 58 Blessings. Your life will never be the same. (Paperback)
(B47) 86 pages..............................$8

 **Wisdom - God's Golden Key To Success**
In this book, Dr. Mike Murdock shares his insight into the Wisdom of God that will remove the veil of ignorance and propel you into the abundant life. (Paperback)
(B71) 67 pages..............................$7

 **The Proverbs 31 Woman**
God's ultimate woman is described in Proverbs 31. Dr. Murdock breaks it down to the pure revelation of these marvelous qualities. (Paperback)
(B49) 68 pages..............................$7

 **One-Minute Businessman's Devotional**
This devotional is packed with success principles from Scripture, inspiring and challenging stories and practical methods for achieving goals. (Paperback)
(B42) 236 pages..............................$10

Remember... God sent His Son, but He left His Book!

Wisdom For Crisis Times

Discover the Wisdom Keys to dealing with tragedies, stress and times of crisis. Secrets that will unlock the questions in the right way to react in life situations. (Paperback) (B40) 118 pages.............................$9

The Double Diamond Principle

This explosive book contains 58 Master Secrets For Total Success, in the life of Jesus that will help you achieve your goals and dreams. (Paperback) (B39) 118 pages.............................$9

The Double Diamond Daily Devotional

This devotional for everyday of the year is filled with dynamics Wisdom Keys and Scriptures for successful leaders and achievers. This volume includes topics on dreams and goals, relationships, miracles, prosperity and more! (Paperback) (B72) 374 pages.............................$10

Wisdom For Winning

The best-selling handbook for achieving success. Every obstacle and pitfall to abundant success is covered in this powerful volume. This book will put in the "Winner's World." If you desire to be successful and happy, this is the book for you! (Paperback) (B01) 280 pages.............................$10

Thirty-One Secrets Of An Unforgettable Woman

Dynamic Wisdom Keys to unveil secrets of one of the greatest Biblical woman in history, Ruth. This book is will change you! (Paperback) (B57) 374 pages.............................$19

Dream Seeds

What do you dream of doing with your life? What you attempt to do if you knew it was impossible to fail? This 118 page book helps you answer these questions and much more! (Paperback) (B11) 118 pages.............................$9

Get Your FREE Copy Of The Wisdom Catalog And FREE Subscription To The *Wisdom Talk* Newsletter Today!

Finally, all of the best materials from Dr. Mike Murdock are now available to you in a beautiful 16-page four-color catalog. Teaching tapes, books, music and gifts laid out for you in an easy-to-read format. Order at your leisure with ease.

The Wisdom Talk newsletter will keep you up to date on the ministry with itineraries, TV & radio schedules, Wisdom articles, new product releases and much more!

Call Toll Free at 1 (888) WISDOM1

41

Order Form

Item No.	Name of Item	Qnty.	Price	Total
#B47	Covenant Of 58 Blessings (Book)		$8.00	$
#B49	Proverbs 31 Woman (Book)		$7.00	$
#B71	Wisdom God's Golden Key (Book)		$7.00	$
#B42	Businessman's Devotional (Book)		$10.00	$
#B11	Dream Seeds (Book)		$9.00	$
#B01	Wisdom For Winning (Book)		$10.00	$
#B39	Double Diamond Principle (Book)		$9.00	$
#B72	Double Diamond Devotional (Book)		$10.00	$
#B40	Wisdom For Crisis Times (Book)		$9.00	$
#B57	Unforgettable Woman (Book)		$9.00	$

SORRY	Add 10% For Shipping	$
NO C.O.D.'S	(Canada add 20%)	$
	Enclosed Is My Seed-Faith Gift For Your Ministry	$
(#DC10)	Total Amount Enclosed	$

Please Print

Name

Address

City

State   Zip

Phone   (Wk)

☐ Check   ☐ Money Order   ☐ Cash

☐ Visa   ☐ MasterCard   ☐ AMEX

Signature_____

Card#

Expiration Date _____

Call for FREE Catalog & FREE Subscription To Newsletter
Wisdom Talk **at 1 (888) WISDOM1**

Mail To:

Mike Murdock

The Wisdom Training Center • P.O. Box 99 • Dallas, TX • 75221

Clip & Mail

NOTES

N O T E S